CONNECTING

Mum

entrepreneurs

MAPPING and ADDING VALUE to your BUSINESS NETWORK

I0041962

Sally A. Curtis

business mums solutions

Published 2015

Publisher: Sally A Curtis - Business Mums Solutions

Graphic Design & Layout: Mélissa Caron – go-Enki.com
Editor: Richard Burian – Richard-Burian.com

Business Development/Growth, Lead Generation, Entrepreneurship, Women's

ISBN: 978-0-9944274-0-3

TABLE OF CONTENTS

What People Say About Sally:

'Sally is incredibly well connected and was able to introduce me to a range of contacts and opportunities outside my standard network. She's professional, friendly and most importantly has an amazing skill to connect people together and develop opportunities you might not have ordinarily seen. A very talented lady!'

- Belinda Jennings,
  Founder & CEO of Mum Central, Australian Baby Bargains and Mum's Pantry

'Sally is exceptional. Her ability to connect the right people at the right time is a gift. Sally is the perfect person for helping to see the power in your own network and to create the best connections for joint ventures and strategic alliances.

'She has an in-depth knowledge of the power and purpose of connecting people in business and the skills and experience to do so in a professional and effective way. Sally is always looking for the greatest win for all parties and her excitement for projects that she is working on is infectious for all those working with her.

'With skills in operations, marketing, sales, strategy, communications, and people management/leadership she is able to seamlessly integrate all aspects and elements of even the most complex venture, deal or alliance in a way that makes it seem easy and effortless.

'Thank you, Sally.'

-Duane Alley,
  Owner at Duane Alley Training

'Sally is indeed a connector. If you commission her to get you connected to whoever you want, your business will fly and you will have more fun and money. She's brilliant.'

-Mike Handcock,
  Chairman at Rock Your Life

'Sally is amazingly creative at making connections that count. She has the ability to see outside the box and is full of enthusiasm and integrity. I just love the way she sorts out problems and trouble shoots.'

-Ruby Johnson,
  Author, Speaker, Facilitator

'Sally is dynamic at building relationships and teams.

'Sally worked as a contractor on a particular project. The role was sales oriented and required prospecting various potential investors, seminars, sales and ensuring delivery of product. Sally is extremely gifted at connecting with others, finding out what makes them tick and then bringing the right people together to make it happen.

'If you are a business owner and want to make your business grow to the next level and beyond, contact Sally who can assess where you are at, offer recommendations and roll up her sleeves to work together with you to make it happen.'

-Jackie Bayly,
Director/Owner at Properties 4U

'Sally was a delight to work with in her role as franchisee development manager at Aussie Farmers Direct. Her input and words of wisdom helped our business through a dark period. She helped me develop the skills I required to ensure ongoing business success.

'I would recommend Sally to anyone who is looking to take their business to the next level.'

-Gerard & Lexie Griggs,
Aussie Farmers Franchisee

'I had the pleasure of working with Sally over the last year. She is my kind of girl, passionate about the little guy, strategic, planned and creative as regards local area marketing, small business and building strong relationships. We worked in a complicated franchisee/franchisor dynamic and the skills and attitude that Sally brought to the table were second to none. I highly recommend her and look forward to collaborating again in the future.'

-Sara Mitchell,
Seasoned professional, passionate advocate and champion for Local Community/SME
and Franchisee challenges/solutions

INTRODUCTION

INTRODUCTION

....

Connecting Mum Entrepreneurs is geared towards mums who are thinking of starting their own business, or who already have their own business set up. The book is filled with detailed information about the key to setting up, owning and operating a successful business of any sort. The advice contained in the book is aimed at mothers who are running a business while taking care of children. While the examples and information in the book refer to mums, they can just as easily apply to dads or to anyone else who is interested in managing their own successful business.

'The richest people in the world look for and build networks.
Everyone else looks for work.'
- Robert Kiyosaki

The key to a successful business is aptly illustrated by the above quote. All successful businesses are based on and defined by the strength of the network that the owner has built up and the number of valuable connections they have.

In essence then, *Connecting Mum Entrepreneurs* is a book not about how to set up a business, because I'm already assuming that you either have your business set up or you already have a good business idea. Whatever stage your business is at, it's probably functioning. Otherwise you wouldn't be doing it!

Sally A. Curtis

business mums solutions

Trainings | Coaching: Personal/Performance | Speaking

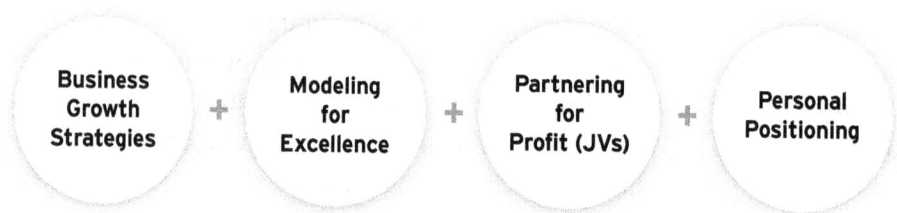

| Business Growth Strategies | + | Modeling for Excellence | + | Partnering for Profit (JVs) | + | Personal Positioning |

AT THE HEART OF WHAT WE DO ARE THESE ACTIVITIES.

At the heart of *Connecting Mum Entrepreneurs* is the phrase, 'It's not what you know, it's who you know.' This is the twist that I bring to the area of business growth. Things happen so much quicker when you know someone that can get your foot in the door... *minimum effort – maximum results*. This is what the book is about. Everything in *Connecting Mum Entrepreneurs* is done through the people we know.

The best way to think of what this book does for your business is like a turbocharger on a car. Your business is the car. If you want your business growth to speed up, then turn the turbo up. To slow down, turn the turbo down.

Connecting Mum Entrepreneurs is also about sharing resources, tools, and stories from other people; sharing tips, training and ideas with my 20 years experience in business. I love great people and great products and will share and endorse them.

This book then, is about how to build up and maintain quality networks as a mum.

There are several parts to building up a valuable business network. These parts will be introduced in the following sections and elaborated throughout the book. Before anything else, learning about business and training are very important. Then, you need to build your networks and begin to market your business. To turbocharge and grow your business, setting up joint ventures is the best way. This is done through getting the most out of events and opportunities, fate meetings with others in business and synergising with them through understanding the essence of people.

a) Learning and Training to Operate a Business

'When the student is ready, the teacher will appear.'
- Mabel Collins, *Light on the Path*

There is a learning and training phase. You might have already taken some courses, read business books, or attended seminars, webinars or workshops to help give you ideas that you can apply to building up your network.

While you are learning and training in your business, the key component is to uncover hidden opportunities. Most of these key opportunities have been there for a long time, but as you have not studied and understood how your networks fit together they were not immediately obvious.

As a mum in business, we already have access to a lot of people, we often just don't know how to approach them or incorporate them successfully into our business. *Connecting Mum Entrepreneurs* is about helping you identify the gold mine within your connection base through increasing the size, quality and strength of those connections.

What is sitting right in front of you, at your fingertips, but hiding in plain sight? The education component of *Connecting Mum Entrepreneurs* focuses on uncovering these opportunities hidden within your connection base. It really is not HOW, but WHO.

b) Building and Marketing Your Business

'You can't be successful when you cling to obsolete situations out of fear. Only when you put yourself out there wholeheartedly can the best opportunities present themselves.'
- Sally Hogshead

The business development phase is done using three different mediums: face-to-face, phone or virtual. Historically this makes sense. Before phones, business was done by meeting people and talking to them (or through letter writing). Before the Internet, most business was done over the phone through sales and cold calling. With the ubiquity of the Internet now, an increasing number of networks are being built using modern devices, software and tools that connect people all over the world.

As a mum, you will want to make use of all three of these methods in tandem with each other to run a successful business venture.

FACE-TO-FACE

Our confidence grows dramatically when we understand who we are, what we have so close at hand and how many opportunities are available to us. This is what this book is all about.

Tips for attending networking face-to-face events:

1. Be confident.

2. Know why you are there and who the types of people you would like to meet are.

3. Ask the organiser or a really friendly person you meet on the way in to point you in the right direction.

4. Once you have done this a few times you will notice other people on the outskirts that are a little nervous. Make them feel comfortable by saying hello and bringing them into a conversation.

5. Practise, practise and practise answering confidently, 'What do you do?'

6. Remember to have fun and be yourself!

> **You can use a worksheet to prepare for networking events or download a FREE version online at BusinessMumsSolutions.com/downloads**
> See page 22 of your *Connecting Mum Entrepreneurs Training Manual* for a worksheet example.

PHONE

Sometimes, even after mums have mapped their network (to be discussed in detail in Chapter 2 – *Mapping Out Your Connections*) and identified the leverage points that are sitting in their Connection Map (again, you will learn in detail what this means in Chapter 2), and have everything they need to rocket their business growth, some people just don't like the phone.

It can be for a whole host of reasons. It seems like such a shame to go through the process of mapping your network out with the intention of expanding your business, to then just stop and go no further.

Here are some tips:

› Be confident, be prepared, have fun, be yourself and be conversational.

› When you are prepared and not just winging it, you OWN confidence! Don't self-sabotage yourself through lack of preparation. You are the master of your actions, thoughts and your outcomes. Preparation is the key!

› Talk as though you are talking or asking a girlfriend for some assistance. Don't get all salesperson-like. Be aware of the voice you use. Be conversational and confident.

VIRTUAL

There are so many great tools available to connect us virtually.

I'm sure you are aware of Facebook and the conversations you can have on that platform. There is a messenger app within Facebook that is also great as you can type messages and even have phone conversations with others. Plus, it's free!

Personally, I love Skype's video chat function and use this with my own coaches and for my clients. It's also great if you want to record the session.

Video recordings are a great way to share information or send thoughts that might get lost in text. Plus, you can record your computer screen and talk through apps such as Screen Recorder, Screen Capture Tool and many other options to choose from.

GoToMeetings is great for phone and presentation style group chat sessions.

c) Events and Opportunities

'Learn to listen. Opportunity could be knocking at your door very softly.'
- Frank Tyger

When you're on the path of collaboration the next step to expanding and leveraging your network of business mums is to attend events where you will meet other people who can provide you with opportunities.

I will add one caution here… it's about attending the right events: the ones where people like you go and where your potential clients go. Attending events for the sake of attending events becomes very costly. If you have a particular interest, which is not served by any local event, then you could create your own Meet Up group.

I have regularly provided mum business owners with a fun and value packed event experience in a synergetic atmosphere, allowing quality connections to occur between true like-minded people. I've done this by bringing unique live events, trainings and speakers to various cities around Australia, providing mums with not only a great connection base and networking opportunities, but also quality, hand picked information that accelerates your business growth.

Today with all the technology we have available to connect I can bring virtual events to my communities and build the connections globally.

Attending events is crucial to finding new opportunities for your business. People like to meet face-to-face, even virtually and most business is done on a trust basis by people who have met each other, sized each other up and decided that the other is someone they would like to do business with.

d) Synergies and Fate Meetings

'Everyone should build their network before they need it.'
- **Dave Delaney**

When you attend these events you might randomly meet people who just 'click' with you.

When you meet the right person at the right time, these are usually described as 'fate meetings'. You don't usually realise this initially; it's later when you join the dots, retrospectively looking back at the path that was created. Alternatively, you can meet someone and hit it off straight away, almost as though you have known each other before or even 'in a past life'.

In my case, the more I worked together with my then partner in business (now my life partner), the more we worked out that we had both very similar goals in life and that our strengths and even our weaknesses complemented each other. We bounced ideas off each other and built on them together. What one started the other was able to finish.

This kind of chance meeting cuts the crap and reduces the time invested. Due to the ease and simplicity of this I have immense fun with my partner in our businesses, doing what we love, and loving what we do.

People always acknowledge this and want to know what we are up to!

Without attending events, you'll never have the chance to come across these 'fate meetings'.

e) The Essence of People

'The world is not changed by people who sort of care.'
- **Sally Hogshead**

One of the rules I have in business is: *the first step to working with someone is understanding their essence.* This means that if their passions are congruent with what they are doing and those two visibly and energetically match, then there is a possibility of working together, whether they are a customer, a partner or an alliance. As I run a business growth company for mums, how could I comfortably recommend and open doors for a person who doesn't fully believe in their business?

This is why I want to find out the essence of everyone I work with and I recommend that you do, too. It makes it so much easier to be able to recommend them to others and grow your network exponentially.

So ask yourself the following questions as you read this book:

1. What is your story behind your sales story?

2. What is your 'WHY?'

3. What is the reason you do what you do, aside from money?

Answer these 3 questions in details and be specific.
See page 29 of your *Connecting Mum Entrepreneurs Training Manual* for this exercise.

---

f) Teamwork and Collaboration: Joint Ventures

'Our success has really been based on partnerships from the very beginning.'
- **Bill Gates**

Over the years, I've sat down with people to work out what Joint Ventures or other collaborative opportunities they have in their networks. For example, when I worked in franchising, I learnt that one of the most successful ways of growing your franchise was to be the local hero in your franchise area.

By aligning and partnering with other businesses in the local community, you can create win-win situations known as 'local area marketing'.

This is the perfect example of teamwork and collaboration of people and businesses working alongside and with each other. The opportunities are endless.

All you need to do is listen effectively to people. Take notice of them and their surroundings and what it is that excites them the most about what they do. It just might align with you and magic could be created.

Listen to learn. Hear to discover. Ask for more information or to catch up again to discuss working together collaboratively.

WHAT IS
Connecting?

WHAT IS *Connecting?*

a) Connecting is More than Communicating

I will point out that I use the word connecting as opposed to networking. For me there is a huge difference energetically around connecting and the global impact that it creates, which I will share with you.

If this isn't connecting, then what is?

Connecting is more than just communicating...

For me it is to look someone in the eyes, with smiling eyes and a warm face. It is to 'feel' you have really connected, stopping for a moment to notice and acknowledge someone and feel their presence and purpose. Connecting is spending time with someone and getting to know them. It is more than just a meeting or a passing, it is a connection. It's a feeling that's so much more than a fleeting glimpse of what might have been.

Most mums in business that I work with have or choose to attend networking events and functions, so you will be able to relate to the following questions around the occurrences at these events.

Have you ever been to a networking event advertised for mums in business where you felt cheated, sold to or even card pimped?

Have you ever felt that people weren't listening to you and just talking about their own problems with their children or partners?

Or have you felt just really, really uncomfortable at an event because you were out of your depth and didn't know what to do?

We all have had those feelings or experiences at one time or another.

Some say they feel gut wrenching nervousness, discomfort and shallowness in the environment, while others feel right at home, smiling, having fun and sharing in the enjoyment.

It is fairly common to have some, if not a lot of resistance about meeting new people in general, let alone at a networking event.

For some, it is the pressure of putting yourself out on a limb, while for others there seems to be an expectation that they need to be the version of themselves that they believe everyone wants to see and not their true self.

From the perspective of a mum just going into business, it could also be an issue of having been the homemaker for years and now, really, for the first time meeting new people and being apprehensive about it.

There are some people that love networking events and yet others absolutely hate them.

WHY is that? How can you BE comfortable and FEEL listened to at an event or networking opportunity?

b) Connecting is Connection

'Networking is more about 'farming' than it is about 'hunting' – it's about cultivating relationships with the people you know.'
- **Dr Ivan Misner, BNI**

Connecting is really the core of everything. Connection is what life is all about.

When we connect, we add value to all those we come in contact with, in every way possible. When we feel connected, we feel more at ease with people, we trust more and we all give more freely, so by connecting more… we give and gather more, creating a ripple effect of connection and connecting. It becomes more than just us; more than just our business.

Our life then feels more exciting and fun and… do I dare say it? Easier!

It is commonly said, 'practice makes perfect'. According to Malcolm Gladwell's book, *Outliers*, it takes most people 10,000 hours to master anything. This can be daunting, but what you actually need to do is bust through your discomfort zone. The more people you talk to at these events, the more people you try to genuinely, honestly connect to, understanding their essence and finding out about them, the better you will get at it.

This is connection!

In *How to Win Friends and Influence People*, Dale Carnegie says, 'Actions speak louder than words, and a smile says, 'I like you. You make me happy. I am glad to see you.' '

So at your next event, walk up to someone with a big smile on your face, say hello, and really get to know them. The more you do this, the better you get!

c) Living an Extraordinarily Connected Life

'The single most important thing is to make people happy. If you are making people happy, as a side effect, they will be happy to open up their wallets and pay you.'
- **Derek Sivers, CD Baby**

But that's just the beginning. Learn to connect with people and really get to know them. Become popular and you will be on the path to living an extraordinarily connected life.

You may not have been the most popular girl in high school and you may not be the most popular woman in your circle of friends today, or in your church, or in your community, but that can and will change.

So how do you live an extraordinarily connected life?

Here is the answer: *it's the art of adding value*. It's creating a culture around a connected life; not in someone else's way but in your UNIQUE way.

Adding value changes everything.

Some of us may not think this is a big deal, so let's have a look at some easy examples to see the lasting impact a connected life can create.

Let's take the enjoyment of the 'family & friends' BBQ experience (something that is really prominent in Australia) into our business worlds. There is no reason why we can't have as much fun in the business world as we do in our personal lives. Time with families and friends can be joyous, entertaining, fun, full of experiences and sharing in a relaxed atmosphere. All this can be taken into our business worlds and professional lives. It is however up to you to do this in your unique way.

We are after all, all human beings and similar in nature.

Our mindset is what impacts the outcomes.

At a friendly BBQ, we are automatically relaxed and in a fun mood. There are no negative expectations or stories we tell ourselves, or thoughts about how others will react or what others may think of us.

It is our perceptions of other people's potential reactions that make us feel uncomfortable in networking or connecting environments.

BBQs have a relaxed atmosphere, we are comfortable straight away, because when friends come together, we are not thinking of how we can sell or get the most out of every person that's there. We are there to be relaxed, have fun, share an experience and add value to those around us.

At your next event, when you are meeting new people, simply lighten up and imagine you're at the family BBQ, talking to your loved ones and your best friends. Of course you don't talk about the same topics... or do you? It depends. But this framework will help you very much to really get the most out of the event and really connect to the people who are there. You will add value to the time they have spent simply because you're laughing and smiling and making them feel like they are having a great time. And you will be having a great time, too.

Adding value is an art form. By being conscious of the art of adding value to others, you create a paradigm shift in the way you think and act. Then you let go, relax and automatically have more fun and create an attractive presence in a relaxed manner.

People will want to be around you and know what you do.

[!] **What topics can help me to add value to the conversation?**
See page 25 of your *Connecting Mum Entrepreneurs Training Manual* for this exercise.

---

d) The 4 Laws of Connecting

'It's very logical: There is proven ROI in doing whatever you can to turn your customers into advocates for your brand or business.
The way to create advocates is to offer superior customer service.'
- Gary Vaynerchuk, *The Thank You Economy*

Connecting to people follows a very simple four-step process. We can call these the four laws of connecting:

LAW 1 - GIVE WITHOUT EXPECTATION

This means no score keeping. Meet people with no expectations in mind. This not only relieves the pressure of high performance, but also means you are there to add value to the person you are meeting. Naturally, what goes around comes around. We are all human beings and we naturally want to help others, it is hard-wired as much as you may not want to admit it, so dig deep and give generously.

Having no expectations allows your mind to be open to any and all opportunities, no blinkers.

Just have fun, ask questions, find out about others and let them talk about themselves. Have no expectations. You will be remembered as someone from the event that cared about them and wanted to know about *them*. That's infinitely more useful than your standard 30-second pitch...

Going in with an agenda means it will be easy to miss other valuable opportunities that may arise, as people tend to focus on and only on their agenda. We have all felt this uncomfortable experience.

> **!** **Write down 5 ways to add value to someone on your connection map with no strings attached.**
> See page 26 of your *Connecting Mum Entrepreneurs Training Manual* for this exercise.

26

LAW 2 – RECIPROCITY

This is a natural phenomenon. When you add massive value to someone, they automatically want to repay the favour and give something back to you. When you give without expectation you create reciprocity.

The amount you get back is usually a lot more than what you give. It's not uncommon for it to come back ten-fold; it may not necessarily come back from the original source of your good deed, but from some other source.

So how do you deal with takers? Since you can't force reciprocity, when do you say enough is enough if the other person is not reciprocating?

We found it best to test and measure, if giving without expectation enhances the relationship and you know that the giving is mutual then we keep going.

If it is a draining process and all the other person does is take, we stop and usually move on from the relationship.

Why would anyone want to be around takers? *Use your instincts as a guide.*

At an event, when you are meeting other mums in business, you have so many opportunities available to you. If someone is being a taker and not giving back what you are giving them after a certain period of time, politely excuse yourself and simply move on and entertain someone else.

> **[!]** **Write down 3 ways to excuse yourself from a taker / energy drainer / inspiration vampire.**
> See page 27 of your *Connecting Mum Entrepreneurs Training Manual* for this exercise.

Story – Don't Miss the Moments

Let me share with you an insight into my life and how communication, confidence and listening have made an impact. Originally I told this story 'Don't Miss the Moments' to an audience at the 'Wise Talk Event' by Trica Karp.

This is a story about a jack-in-the-box and a rubbish tip.

Image an old style, bright, springy child's toy. It's a jack-in-the-box that has a little handle on the side that you wind up, waiting for the lid to go, 'click'. Then, out explodes a larger than life, smiling, happy clown. It bounces around, from side to side; captivating imaginations and making everyone smile and laugh. You feel the joy.

Now let's stroll around the outskirts of a rubbish tip.

It's a really hot day, so the smells are thick and pungent. You feel like you're pushing through the muck in the air. Gazing out over the vastness of the rubbish tip, you see hundreds and hundreds of metres of household rubbish, items no longer wanted, all decaying.

The jack-in-the-box has become part of that rubbish tip. Dented, stinky, unhappy, its colours faded to shades of grey, lifeless. Its smile has gone. It can no longer hold its own attention, let alone anyone else's.

If you haven't already guessed, that jack-in-the-box was the life I had created at an earlier point in my life. During that time I missed so many moments. Being a workaholic was my way to avoid an unhappy marriage. I was numb, disengaged and lifeless. I was in denial.

I was missing connection with myself, my family and all the moments that could have been shared.

Thankfully, I woke up. I worked on myself, left a long-term marriage and created a new life. It was traumatic for us all. Over time Rory, my son who was five at the time, seemed to become more and more withdrawn. He was looking like the jack-in-the-box.

I knew I needed to rebuild our relationship in a new way and really connect.

It's funny how little gifts come packaged when you are awake to receive them. I was sitting in a sales training not really enjoying it. I felt the techniques were manipulative. 'Mirroring, pretending to listen by repeating the last word the person said. Blah, blah.'

However, I decided to test it, in a kinder way, with Rory by echoing him. Our normal after school conversation would go like this:

Me: *'What did you do today?'*

Rory: *'Painting.'*

Me: *'What else?'*

Rory: *'Can't remember.'*

END OF CONVERSATION.

Instead, I began to echo his last words. This is what happened:

Me: *'What did you do today?'*

Rory: *'Painting.'*

Me: *'Painting?'*

Rory: *'Yes, we did a picture of a rainbow.*

Me: *'Rainbow?'*

Rory: *'Yes, it was all colours, purple, green, red, blue, orange, yellow.'*

Me: *'Yellow?'*

Rory: 'Yes, yellow is my favourite colour.'

Me: 'Favourite colour?'

Rory: 'Yes, 'cause its like gold, gold is precious, did you know that?'

Me: 'Precious?'

Rory: 'Yes, like silver, diamonds, rubies all those sorts of things you would find in a pirate's chest.'

Me: 'Pirate's chest?'

Rory: 'Yes, we learnt about pirates today in the library, we read a book and pretended to be characters from it.'

Me: 'Characters?'

That conversation lasted longer than the car ride home and the connection I got with my Rory was enormous. He felt valued; I wasn't just asking him questions. I participated in his journey of learning and experiencing.

* * *

This change in participation has overflowed to other areas. As a consultant working from home, I lived on my mobile phone and computer. I'm not sure who ruled whom. I'd often pop into my office just to quickly check in and make sure I was still important. Rory followed me in one day, sat on the floor alongside me looked up and said, 'You don't ever play with me.'

I turned off the phone and shut the office door. We played.

Dinnertime has become an extension of us all sharing our experiences. Phones, TV and all technology stay off. We share some time together over a meal. We ask, 'What was your highlight of the day?' We have done this for several years now and magic happens.

Occasionally Rory will now add a lowlight, a struggle or a frustration. As a family we get to discover more of what's happening in his world and assist if needed.

Small steps add up to great things.

A few nights ago as I tucked him into bed, he asked, 'So mum, what's really happening in your world?' He had seen that I had my brave face on, so we talked.

Moments of honesty just happen.

We all ride roller coasters in life; we all have ups and downs. Challenges continue and that's okay.

Rory was sitting at the dinner table doing his homework and I was cooking tea. He seemed unusually still, but agitated at the same time. His head was in his hand; he was hunched over. Then it happened. He fell to the floor in a shaking, sobbing teary mess. A stressed out, sobbing mess... over homework!

He was nine the first time it happened.

* * *

My point here is twofold:

1) No matter how good your communication gets in your household, challenges will always show up and kids need to understand that's okay.

2) Our kids learn from us; they watch and feel us. Even when you don't think they do. Rory had just re-enacted a scene from my previous life, from when he was only about three, which he never actually saw.

I was able to talk through this with Rory and share some tools to help him. However a Ted Talk impacted him the most. He watched Amy Cuddy's, *Your Body Language Shapes Who You Are.*

(Link: www.ted.com/talks/amy_cuddy_your_body_language_shapes_who_you_are)

Cuddy is a social psychologist whose research on body language reveals that we can change other people's perceptions – and our own – simply by changing body postures.

Low power poses: hunched over, head in hand.

High power poses: Victory Vs, which we see sporting stars do.

She explains what happens chemically and physically in the body for the two poses.

Rory was captivated by it.

Here's a strategy we developed for times when he is feeling stressed or afraid to ask for help whilst he's at school.

Now standing up in the middle of the class doing full Victory Vs would be a challenge for Rory.

Remember back to your early dating years when the boys would pretend to yawn to put their arms around their girls.

I shared that with Rory. Not that he liked the girl part.

However, a harmless yawning stretch is okay in class. We added a little extra jiggle. I say extra, because Rory doesn't sit still usually. This is the, 'I need to go to the loo' move. A purposeful jiggle that has momentum, which builds up to a yawn, that's Victorious.

It looks a bit silly, but it works. It totally changes how you feel and it can be done anywhere. It turbo boosts confidence. Check out Amy Cuddy's TED talk and see for yourself.

To boost my confidence as a parent with a son fast approaching teenage years, I keep a little book to capture our family moments to laugh at later.

Through all of this I have learnt to participate in life and family again. The honest communication rippled over to our new families, giving us two more extended families to share moments with.

I beg you, don't be a lifeless jack-in-the-box. You create the moments. You may need to set the example. Your family needs you, you need you and your kids need you.

Don't miss the moments; make more of them!

....

LAW 3 - ABUNDANCE

Opportunities are like busses; there is always another one coming. Most of the opportunities in life are hidden in plain sight, waiting to be uncovered. There are two sides to every coin.

One is where everything is scarce and there is not enough of anything. The other is a world full of possibilities, a constant flow of everything you need. *You just need to tap into it.*

Which side of life and business are you looking at most of the time?

If you are looking at the dark/scarce side, try the other one and ask, 'Where can I find what I am looking for? Who or what do I already have at my fingertips within my current connections?'

When you think about every person in your network and think about what possibilities you could achieve with them, you quickly find out more than you could ever have imagined.

LAW 4 - LOVE

'The only way to do great work is to love what you do.'
- **Steve Jobs**

If you haven't found it yet, keep looking and don't settle.

The only way to do great work is to love what you do. We have all been around people who feel draining and have negative energy, because they hate what they are doing. It's in their facial expressions, personal presentation, conversations and tone of voice. This isn't about faking it to sell some product or services; it is about being passionate about what you do.

The best way to look at this is to find a kid that is doing something they absolutely love. My son Rory loves Super Heroes. It is a dead giveaway when he sees them. His eyes open wide, there is a huge grin on his face, he begins to talk at the speed of light and visibly vibrates.

In the grown up world, people are attracted to this kind of reaction in a big way. Not many people really love what they do, so when you are having an absolute blast doing what you love, it shows big time! It draws people to you in droves. They want to know what you are on!

Speak from the heart. You will stick out like a sore thumb and your attitude will be deeply appreciated. When you do this you are not selling, you are simply sharing what you are passionate about and letting others decide if it resonates with them as well.

! **What are my passions?**
See page 28 of your *Connecting Mum Entrepreneurs Training Manual* for this exercise.

e) The Story Behind the Sales Story

'There is a divine purpose behind everything – and therefore a divine presence in everything.'
- **Neale Donald Walsch**

Often when you go to a networking event, you will come across people who are only in it for themselves.

Most people try and sell their product or service without any emotional involvement to what they do. Life without passion and excitement is an empty shell, so why bother?

Get involved! Be passionate and if you can't be passionate about what you are involved in at the moment, then find something else where you can be! This is imperative. The story behind the sales story is your 'WHY'.

Why do you do what you do? Gone are the days where we are happy to hear a sales pitch on a new product, or listen to a telemarketer on the other end of a phone with a sales pitch that they themselves don't care less about. An increasingly large proportion of the population is sick of this tacky way of supposedly connecting. People are looking for a story; they are looking for a reason behind what you are doing, something they can resonate with and feel.

They are looking for a *True Connection*.

I believe a *True Connection* is created by two main things. There are a lot of others, but two main ones: the *essence of people* and *your own uniqueness*.

! **What are my WHYs?**
See page 29 of your *Connecting Mum Entrepreneurs Training Manual* for this exercise.

MAPPING OUT
your Connections

MAPPING OUT *your* Connections

'A well designed and managed network will exponentially earn more, create more, than a hard working individual.'
- **Robert Kiyosaki**

A crucial piece of the puzzle for any woman in business is to work out how she can best utilise her existing network. Many people's networks are not very organised. Sure, we are all connected to people on Facebook, LinkedIn and Twitter and we all go to a variety of community groups, clubs and churches. Our children have friends and we might be friends with their parents. We know the local football or netball coach and through him or her we know a lot more other people. We have hairdressers, dentists and doctors. We know even more people through them.

But very few people have taken the time to put it all down in a written or visual form so it's easier to understand and process. The following chapter will teach you how to create your connection map and leverage it to your success as a mum business owner.

a) What is a Connection Map?

A connection map is simply the idea of putting down in a written or visual form every person that you know and to map out the way that you are connected to them.

Your connection map is unique. It is like no other person's connection map. At the centre of your map you will sit and everyone else you know will be close to you on the map or far away from you. Your map will have lines connecting people. When it's completed the whole thing looks like a large tree with many branches. It's almost like a family tree, but for your network.

The following sections will take you step by step through the process of mapping out your network. More importantly, these sections will teach you how to identify leverage points and circles of influence in your network so you can grow your business exponentially faster than the traditional methods.

The process will show you:

› What to look for when growing your business through connections;

› Different ways of building you *Connection Map*;

› Why it is so much faster to do it this way; and

› How you can mix and match people's gifts and passions to make life so much easier in your business.

b) Starting Blocks to Your Connection Map

Let's start things off by putting some context behind what we are about to learn together.

'IT'S NOT WHAT YOU KNOW, IT'S WHO YOU KNOW'.

Even though this phrase is well known, very few people use this concept as a key part of their business growth plans. Why? We found the answer after helping people out with countless *Connection Maps*.

Over and over again, it became clear that people take for granted two things:

› Who they have at their fingertips; and

› What these people are great at.

Once people allow someone with a fresh perspective to show them their value and how significant it really is in the eyes of everyone else, the puzzle pieces and the way they fit together become very clear.

Those two, easily missed leverage points are what makes the difference when growing your business.

> **[!] Name 5 to 10 people who are close to you and what they're great at.**
> See page 31 of your *Connecting Mum Entrepreneurs Training Manual* for this exercise.

c) A Snapshot of Your Current Network

'The population of the Earth is closer together now than they have ever been before (...) using no more than five individuals, one of whom is a personal acquaintance, he could contact the selected individual using nothing except the network of personal acquaintances.'
- Frigyes Karinthy

A Network: *Not necessarily customers or clients, but a network of people who know, like and trust you. They may never buy from you, but you are always in the back of their mind because they are people that want and will help you to succeed.*

A Connection: *Anyone you have met, no matter how briefly.*
There are several different strengths of connections, which will be revealed later.

Before we start, we need to know where you are at present; we need to take a snapshot. Once you know this, we have something solid to build on. Without it, everything can become a blur, not to mention difficult to measure results. Knowing where you are starting from is very important in determining what to do to reach your destination.

Before you start mapping out your network on paper, think about whom you know. It's easiest to imagine this process in a series of concentric circles. Start with your immediate family, your partner's family, your children's friends, their parents, the school your children attend, your friends and so on. Just imagine all the people you must know, directly or indirectly. Is it hundreds? Is it more than a thousand? You would be surprised!

TAKE A SNAPSHOT OF YOUR NETWORK

The questions below will give you a snapshot of your network as it is right now:

1. How many people do you know at the moment? Take a quick guess?

2. How do you go about generating business at the moment? Networking, Direct Mail, Email Marketing, etc.?

3. How often do you keep in touch with your connections, customers and members of your databases? Daily, weekly, monthly, annually, etc.?

4. How much do you spend monthly on generating leads and new business-growth opportunities?

5. When you go to a networking event and receive a business card from someone, what do you do with it? What happens after the event?

6. Out of every 10 customers, how many on average originate from your network?

7. When you think of the people you know (i.e. the people in you network) do you pre-judge them by saying 'they wouldn't buy from me/help me'?

[!] **Fill the questionnaire in your manual!**
See page 32 of your *Connecting Mum Entrepreneurs Training Manual* for this exercise.

Top Tip - Visual Elements and Tools for Keeping Tabs on Your Network

1) I keep all the business cards that I receive in a big lever arch binder, inserting them into plastic sleeves. This is an old school way of keeping track of the people you meet and organising the business cards that you are given at connecting events.

2) If you prefer to use modern technology, iPhones and Androids have many apps available that will let you scan and store pictures of business cards you receive electronically. You'll be able to access the information from them anywhere and the software will convert the text on the image to text that goes straight into your contacts on the phone.

3) You can also use a big artist board to put your network in a more permanent and immediately obvious form when you are done mapping it out in your office. This is a powerful visual representation that will allow you to remember where everyone fits in. If you frequently update your network then you can use cards that you stick to a board instead of printing out a poster of your network.

MARKET STATISTICS FOR COMPARISON

A cross section of people, based on my surveys, only believes they know 100-200 people.

In most cases, these numbers are tripled by using and actioning the process we are about to go through.

The average 18-year-old knows 1,000 people!

Don't worry if your connection numbers are a little low at the moment, *Connecting Mum Entrepreneurs* was written to help you explode your network.

The human brain can only store 7-9 pieces of information at any given time. This is why when it comes to thinking about how many connections we have we can only recall the people closest to us and people we have recently met.

RORY'S CONNECTION MAP

I have an 11-year-old son, Rory. I put together a snapshot of his network when he was 5 ½ years old. He has been to childcare, kindergarten and recently started school. He also goes to swimming and karate lessons so will no doubt be similar to your own children or children you know. Below this section is a *Connection Map* of Rory's network. Let's check it out and see how it works.

I have mapped Rory's network out using a basic style of mind mapping. I start with a central idea and then write down the different areas of his life. From there we list the various people in those different areas.

What will a 10% increase in Rory's connection database mean to him? At the moment it doesn't mean much as we don't know whom he knows. Let me explain.

Starting at the top and moving around clockwise, the connections quickly mount up; just in the first three areas there are over sixty people. Taking into account everyone he knows, whether he has made those connections as friends or through association, he still knows them.

Before you know it, he has 465 connections!

Who could he call if he wants help on something? He has 465 choices. This is where you can start to see how an 18-year-old knows over 1,000 people, when you factor in that he will finish high school in six or so years. BUT it doesn't matter how large your network is if you aren't aware of who is in it.

RORY'S CONNECTION MAP

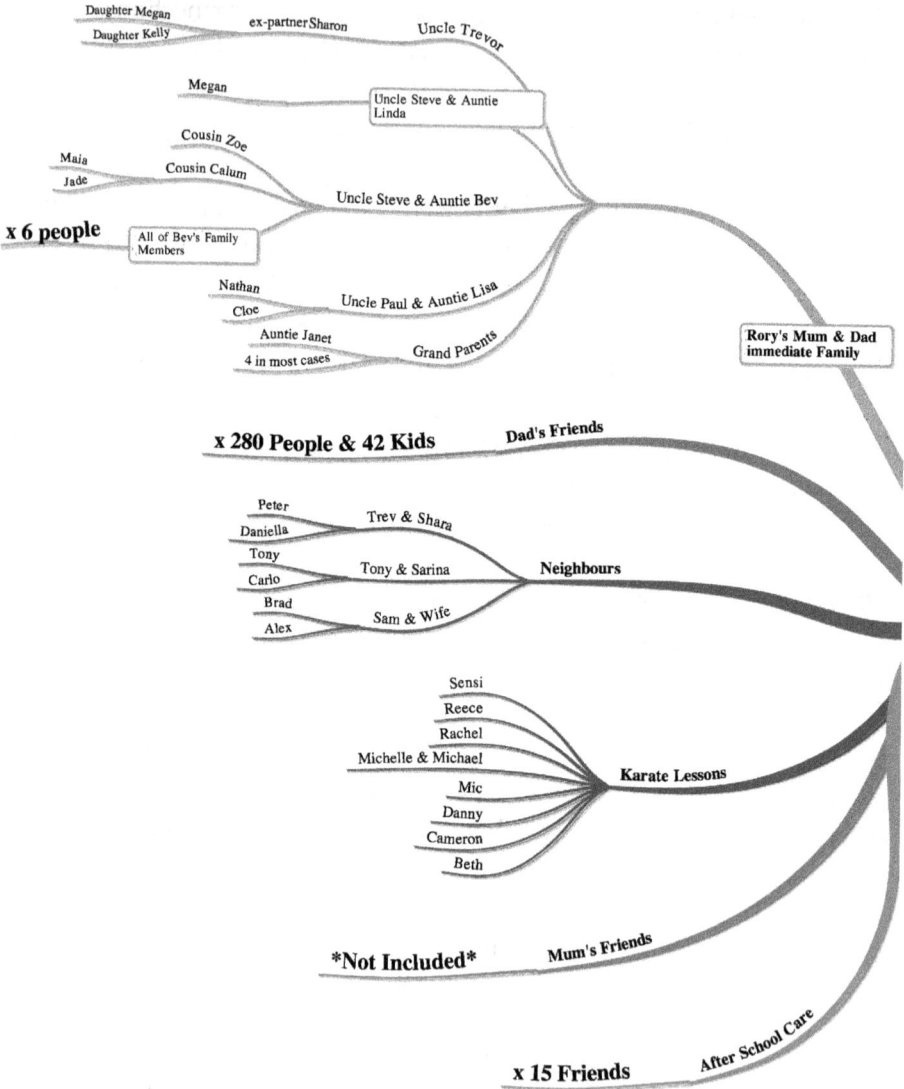

Daughter Megan

Daughter Kelly

ex-partner Sharon

Uncle Trevor

Megan

Uncle Steve & Auntie Linda

Cousin Zoe

Maia

Jade

Cousin Calum

Uncle Steve & Auntie Bev

x 6 people

All of Bev's Family Members

Nathan

Cloe

Uncle Paul & Auntie Lisa

Auntie Janet

4 in most cases

Grand Parents

Rory's Mum & Dad immediate Family

x 280 People & 42 Kids

Dad's Friends

Peter

Daniella

Trev & Shara

Tony

Carlo

Tony & Sarina

Neighbours

Brad

Alex

Sam & Wife

Sensi

Reece

Rachel

Michelle & Michael

Mic

Danny

Cameron

Beth

Karate Lessons

Not Included

Mum's Friends

x 15 Friends

After School Care

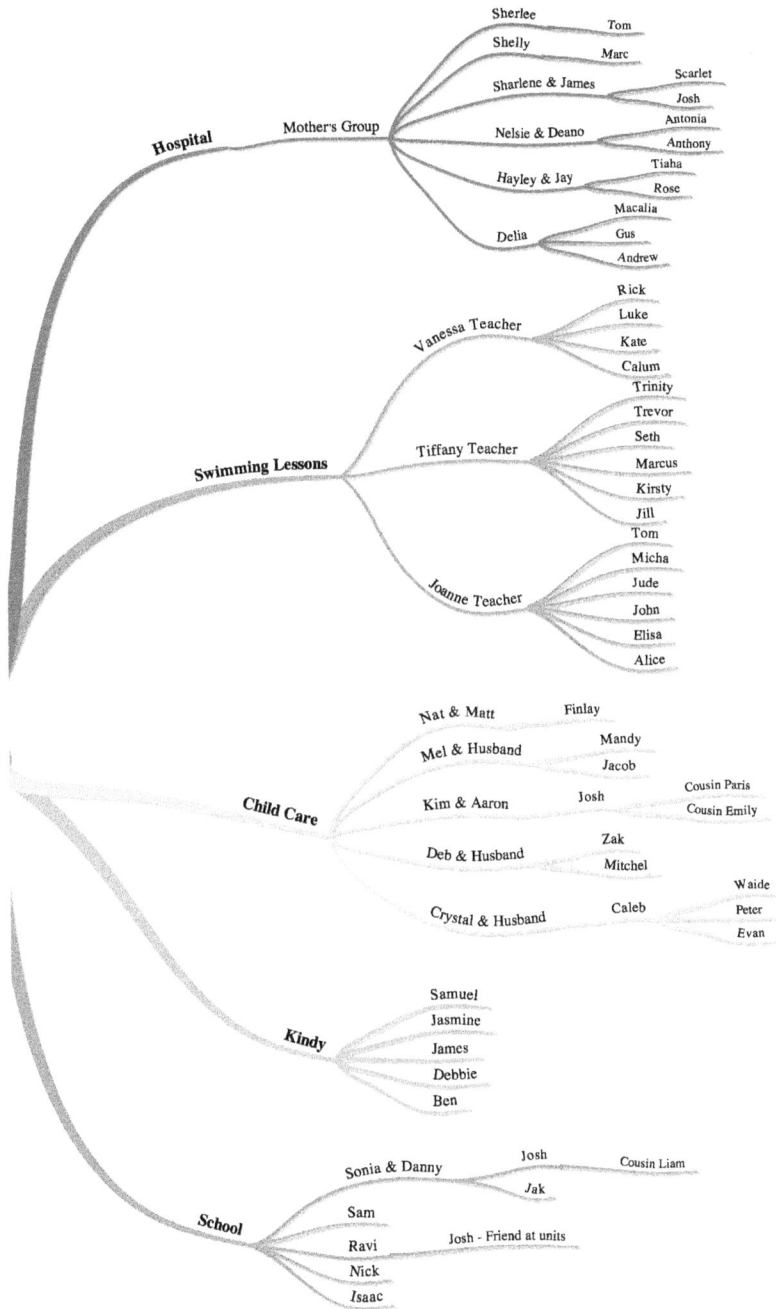

Hospital
Mother's Group
- Sherlee
  - Tom
- Shelly
  - Marc
- Sharlene & James
  - Scarlet
  - Josh
- Nelsie & Deano
  - Antonia
  - Anthony
- Hayley & Jay
  - Tiaha
  - Rose
- Delia
  - Macalia
  - Gus
  - Andrew

Swimming Lessons
- Vanessa Teacher
  - Rick
  - Luke
  - Kate
  - Calum
- Tiffany Teacher
  - Trinity
  - Trevor
  - Seth
  - Marcus
  - Kirsty
  - Jill
  - Tom
- Joanne Teacher
  - Micha
  - Jude
  - John
  - Elisa
  - Alice

Child Care
- Nat & Matt
  - Finlay
- Mel & Husband
  - Mandy
  - Jacob
- Kim & Aaron
  - Josh
    - Cousin Paris
    - Cousin Emily
- Deb & Husband
  - Zak
  - Mitchel
- Crystal & Husband
  - Caleb
    - Waide
    - Peter
    - Evan

Kindy
- Samuel
- Jasmine
- James
- Debbie
- Ben

School
- Sonia & Danny
  - Josh
    - Cousin Liam
  - Jak
- Sam
- Ravi
  - Josh - Friend at units
- Nick
- Isaac

d) Different Styles of Mind Mapping

'The ladder of success is best climbed by stepping on the rungs of opportunity.'
- **Ayn Rand**

Before you do the mind mapping section, get comfortable. Grab a tea or coffee and get relaxed. Flop onto your favourite chair or bed – anywhere that you can think clearly.

First, you have two choices of how you compile your Connection Map:

1. Individual Connections: recommended for people with Connections under 1,000.

2. Group Connections: recommended for people with Connections in excess of 1,000.

Re-think and estimate how many connections you have and decide which of the above choices you'll use to note down your *Connection Map*.

Secondly, there are three ways you can actually draw your *Connection Map*. Through facilitating sessions where people map out their networks, I have found that people have certain tendencies. It's best to work out which one works best for you up front, so you are comfortable with your map when you have finished. The three tendencies are:

1. **Spatial**

2. **Lists**

3. **Mixture of both**

If you look back at Rory's mind map, I used *spatial* mind mapping. This means that the branches and nodes are spaced out wherever they should naturally go. This spatial style is often the choice for creative people. One thing to be aware of is that if you have a lot of connections, spatial mind maps can get crowded.

List mind maps are often used by more analytical people that prefer their map neat, tidy and laid out row by row so they can easily see who is who.

Having a *mixture of both* works well for anyone in between very creative and very analytical. Mixed connection maps contain branches and nodes, but underneath each node there are lists of people.

I have included an example of each on the following pages. The most important thing when deciding which one to choose is that you are comfortable with it. The people that are not comfortable with it to start with are never comfortable with their map at the end. Even worse, they don't use their map as much, because it doesn't work like their brain does. As a result it is always a strain to look at it.

EXAMPLE OF *SPATIAL* MIND MAPPING
(PLEASE REFER TO RORY'S CONNECTION MAP)

EXAMPLE OF *LIST* MIND MAPPING

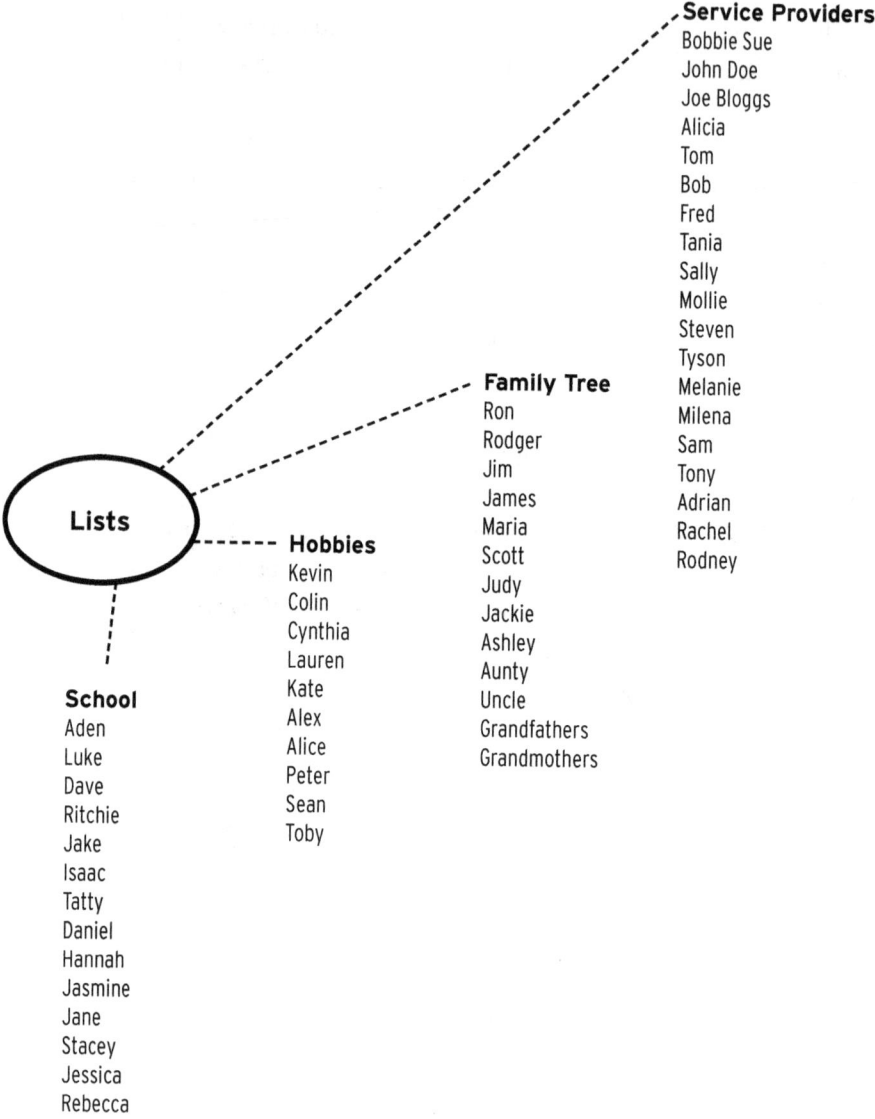

Service Providers
Bobbie Sue
John Doe
Joe Bloggs
Alicia
Tom
Bob
Fred
Tania
Sally
Mollie
Steven
Tyson
Melanie
Milena
Sam
Tony
Adrian
Rachel
Rodney

Family Tree
Ron
Rodger
Jim
James
Maria
Scott
Judy
Jackie
Ashley
Aunty
Uncle
Grandfathers
Grandmothers

Lists

Hobbies
Kevin
Colin
Cynthia
Lauren
Kate
Alex
Alice
Peter
Sean
Toby

School
Aden
Luke
Dave
Ritchie
Jake
Isaac
Tatty
Daniel
Hannah
Jasmine
Jane
Stacey
Jessica
Rebecca

EXAMPLE OF *MIXED* MIND MAPPING

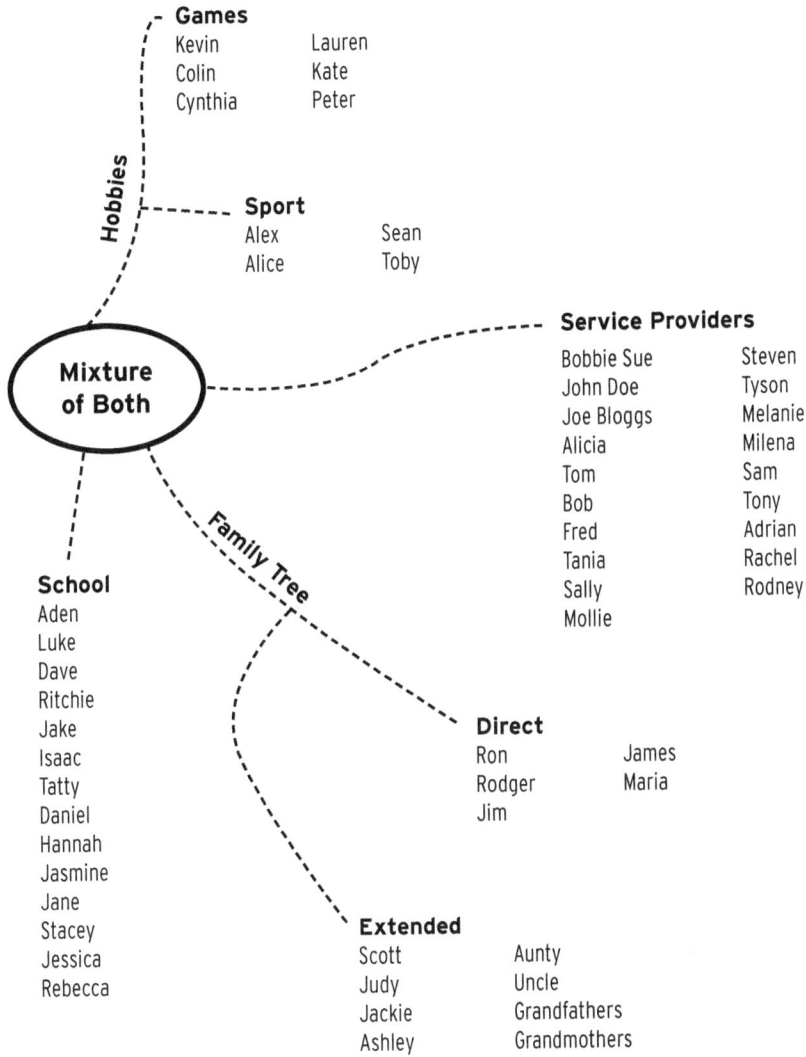

Games
Kevin   Lauren
Colin   Kate
Cynthia Peter

Hobbies

Sport
Alex   Sean
Alice   Toby

Mixture of Both

Service Providers
Bobbie Sue   Steven
John Doe   Tyson
Joe Bloggs   Melanie
Alicia   Milena
Tom   Sam
Bob   Tony
Fred   Adrian
Tania   Rachel
Sally   Rodney
Mollie

Family Tree

School
Aden
Luke
Dave
Ritchie
Jake
Isaac
Tatty
Daniel
Hannah
Jasmine
Jane
Stacey
Jessica
Rebecca

Direct
Ron   James
Rodger   Maria
Jim

Extended
Scott   Aunty
Judy   Uncle
Jackie   Grandfathers
Ashley   Grandmothers

Now you have decided which type and style of mind mapping you are going to use you can get down to business. It is at this point you need to take your blinkers off. Every time I've helped somebody map their network, the number one stumbling block, by a large margin, was pre-judging. This is where the voice inside your head says, 'they wouldn't be interested in me'. Or, 'I don't know them well enough to put them on my map'. Or, 'that person might not be able to help me, so I'll leave them off my map at this stage'. Or, 'that person wouldn't help me'. Remember back to the definition of a network at the start of this Chapter.

A Network: *Not necessarily customers or clients, but a network of people who know, like and trust you. They may never buy from you, but you are always in the back of their mind because they are people that want and will help you to succeed.*

Be careful of pre-judging people because the only person you are short-changing is yourself. There just might be an opportunity with that person, if you look at it from a different perspective, even their perspective. The mapping process is about getting names out of your head and into your Connection Map. At this stage we are not looking at the quality of those names, it's just about the names at this point.

e) Segment Your Life

'The real voyage of discovery consists not in seeking new landscapes but in having new eyes.'
- Marcel Proust

It can be difficult to just begin writing down hundreds, or even thousands of names with no plan! Just like Rory did with his Network, he first wrote down the different aspects of his life. It is time for you to do the same.

At the beginning of this chapter I asked you to think for a few moments about some of the different areas of your life and the people that are in these areas. On the next few pages there is a sample mind map that will give you some ideas (the ones most often used when we facilitate the program), but it is by no means an exhaustive list. If you have an area of your life that isn't on the list, by all means write it down.

> **Write down the different areas of your life.**
> **It could be based on friends, family, workplace, children's friends, schools, partner's friends, family, etc.**
> See page 34 of your *Connecting Mum Entrepreneurs Training Manual* for this exercise.

Great! You now have the basis for your Connection Map. These different areas of your life will form the branches that sprout out from your central node.

Draw your central node (circle in the middle of the page) and come up with a name for your network. If you are feeling a bit unimaginative, then you might want to call it 'My Network', 'The Connected Business Mum' or for the more creatively inclined 'It's not what you know, it's who you know!' Put the name you choose into the central point.

Now, let's work on your first area. Using the style of mind mapping you chose, draw the first branch from the central point outwards and label it as your first area.

For the people doing the list style connection map, write down as many people as you can think of in that particular area of your life. Remember it is not about the quality of the connections at this stage it is only about getting all of names out of your head and onto paper. Because we often find that one name leads to another and then the name that can really make a difference to you; but you would miss this if you didn't start with the first name.

To give you a head start we have included a whole bunch of questions that should get the creative juices flowing. Remember not to pre-judge anyone!

Repeat this process with all the different segments you listed out on the previous page. One by one, go around and write down as many names as you can within each segment.

f) Mind Map Questions

'Your big opportunity may be where you are right now.'
- **Napoleon Hill**

Ask the following questions to mentally map your networks. Write down the answers beside each point:

> **!** **You will find a complete questionnaire in your Training Manual!**
> See page 36 of your *Connecting Mum Entrepreneurs Training Manual* for this exercise.

Country I was born in:

a) Who are my relatives where I was born?

b) Who do I receive Christmas cards and letters from overseas?

c) Where I work?
   Do they have an international presence?
   Who do I know in that international arena?

d) Who do I speak to on Facebook regularly?

e) Who sent me an invitation recently?

f) Who has an upcoming birthday, engagement, wedding or other special day?

2. Country I now live in:

a) Who are my friends where I now live?

b) Who are my relatives where I live now?

c) Who do I get Christmas cards, letters, postcards or E-cards from?

d) Who are my top 10 closest friends?

e) Who do I go on holidays with?

f) Who do I know interstate?

g) Who do I know really well in business that is interstate?

h) Who are my 'once in a blue moon' contacts?

3. Employment:

a) How many companies have I worked for?
   Who are the people I know at each company?

b) Who do I work with now?

c) Who are all the people I know at work?

d) Who do I know in associations and unions I am a member of?

e) Am I a member of a social club?
   Who do I know there?

f) Am I an SME (subject matter expert) at work?
   Who turns to me for help?

g) Who do I see in the lift, car park, train or bus on the way to work?

4. Family tree:

a) Who is in my immediate family? Brothers, sisters, parents?

b) How many in-laws have I had?

c) Who are my aunties, uncles, cousins, second cousins
   and whom are they married to?

5. Hobbies:

a) What hobbies have I had?
   Who have I known within each hobby I have had?

b) What hobbies have my kids and partner(s) had?

c) What groups are associated with my hobbies?

d) How do my groups/hobbyists communicate with each other?
   Who do I communicate with?

e) Is my hobby nationally or globally popular?
   Who do I know within these areas or who can introduce me to these areas?

6. Neighbours:

a) How many addresses have I had?
   Who did I live next to at each address?

b) How many people were there at each of theses addresses?

7. Own business:

a) Who were/are my suppliers?

b) Who were/are my clients?

c) Who were/are my distributors?

d) Who were/are the reps that see me?

e) Who did I advertise with?

f) Who were/are my staff members?

g) Who were/are my service providers?

h) Have I had previous businesses?
   Who were my employees, clients, suppliers?

i) Who are the people whose business cards are most likely in a pile in my office somewhere?

8. Our kids' contacts:

When you are writing down your kids' contacts, it is not about whom your kids talk to, but whom you talk to while you are in your kids' environment.
(e.g. who do you speak to when you are watching your son play sport?)

a) Refer to Rory's network for ideas.

b) Who are my child's best friends and their family members? Who are their parents?

c) Who does my child speak to on social media? Who are their parents?

d) How many sports are my kids involved in (coaching, music, dance)? Who are the parents in each of these activities?

9. Schooling:

a) Where did I go to school and who was in my class?

b) Who do I still see from kindergarten, primary- and secondary school?

c) Who do I / did I know at TAFE or University?

d) While at school, who impacted me the most? (These can be great teachers as well.)

10. Service Providers:

a) Who cuts my hair?

b) Who makes my lunch everyday?

c) Who do I buy my cappuccinos from?

d) What trades or maintenance do I use?

e) Girls: who makes me look beautiful? (Waxing, chiropractor, massage.)

f) Guys: where do I catch up with my mates?

11. Social Media Networks:

a) What social media do I use?
   Who are my friends on Social Media?

b) What groups or pages am I a member of?
   Who is also a fan of those groups and pages?

c) Who do I communicate with regularly?

12. Sport:

a) What sports do I do? Who are the people in them?

b) Who did I hang around the playground with, as a kid?

c) What sports have I played and who were (are) my teammates?

d) Who was my favourite coach?

e) What was my favourite activity as a kid?
   Who did I play with?

f) Who do I know that is big into sports?

13. Your mobile contacts:

a) Who is in my mobile phone?

b) Who is in my email contact list?

c) Who do I receive a newsletter from?

Once you have finished, count up all the people on your list.

Hold on to your seat!

Now that you have the bulk of your Connection Network completed, we can move onto discovering and homing in on the leverage points in your network.

g) Determine the Quality of Your Connections

'We each have the potential to do something beyond our wildest imagination.
As long as we're prepared to make it happen.'
- **Sally Hogshead**

So far you have written down everyone you know, without taking into account how well you know them. It's time to find out how strong your current connections are. There are 5 stages of connections. These 5 stages make up the flow of a relationship from first meeting to becoming a key part of your life.

HOW TO INCREASE THE STRENGTH OF YOUR CONNECTIONS

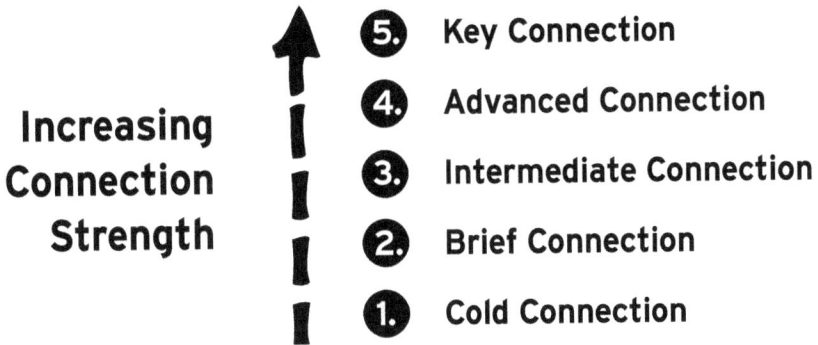

Increasing Connection Strength ↑

5. **Key Connection**

4. **Advanced Connection**

3. **Intermediate Connection**

2. **Brief Connection**

1. **Cold Connection**

DEFINITIONS

5. Key Connection: This is what you are aiming for. You know them and they know you nearly inside out. These are the people who turn to you and who you turn to when help is needed. It might be in a business, financially or anything personal as well. These are the people who you would go out of your way for and vice versa, that is how strong the rapport is. At this stage you can move forward together and blitz anything and everything life throws at you! These are the people that often become mentors and trusted allies.

4. Advanced Connection: You know this person really well. They are usually great friends with a very high level of rapport. If you are having a party, a BBQ or drinks, they are on the invite list. You don't have to have known them for long, but you do have to know them well and feel really comfortable with them. You would characterise these people as best friends

3. Intermediate Connection: This is the stage everyone is familiar with. It is the stage where you call people 'friends'. You are comfortable with these people, you know them quite well. You know what they do, why they do it, and what their passions are.

2. Brief Connection: You may have seen these people a few times here and there, but you don't know much about them. You may know roughly what they do and who they are, but haven't really had the opportunity to properly connect. You might find them interesting and would like to know out more about them.

1. Cold Connection: Someone you have never met. You know nothing about them and vice versa. If you don't know how to add value to what they do then they are usually a cold connection.

Your network has a whole host of connections, each in one of the 5 levels. Most of your connections will be 3s, 4s and 5s, which are intermediate, advanced, or key. These are people you have varying degrees of rapport with. Friendship and trust are already established.

As you probably guessed, 1s and 2s are the hardest to break through. They are known as icebreakers, because it takes a lot of time, energy and rapport to move them onto 3s, 4s and 5s. Cold and Brief connections cause people the most grief and stress as they can be time intensive, because you are building the relationship foundation.

Having seen this, who do you think the target is for most businesses through their advertising and marketing? Is it the 3s, 4s, 5s or the 1s and 2s?

That's right, the main focus is often on 1s and 2s, where the most stress and grief is. Where do you think the majority of businesses spend most of their time and money? 3s-5s are the most cost effective; it's where you can get down to business! But this is not usually where most of the budget goes.

You network will most likely have lots and lots of 3s, 4s and 5s. The hardest work has already been done.

If you worked mainly through 3s, 4s and 5s, would that save a lot of time and energy? Absolutely! So why do so many people, possibly including you, ignore it? It's just one of those things we take for granted, and it's never brought to our full attention.

Connections make growing your business so much easier. We aren't suggesting that every single thing needs to be done through connections. What we are suggesting is that you could save yourself an enormous amount of time, energy and money if you look to your Connection Network first.

So where do your current connections sit?

> **!** Look back at your Connection Map and find the people that fit into the Key Connection and Advanced Connection areas.
> Mark their names by either putting a 5 or a 4 next to them, or highlighting them in some way that makes sense to you.
> See page 72 of your *Connecting Mum Entrepreneurs Training Manual* for this exercise.

MINIMUM EFFORT - MAXIMUM RESULTS

When people start out in business, they immediately look for new leads... new potential clients. This starts the ball rolling at Number 1: *Cold Connections*. If you look at your current connection list you are already at Number 3 or 4 with most of them. If you start at Number 1 you need to move through two stages before the connection has the strength you already have with your current contacts. Why not start at Number 3 when you are searching for something and short cut the process? It could be looking for leads, a personal trainer, employees or someone with specialist knowledge who can help you solve a problem.

This saves you time, money and energy. It takes all the hard work out, so all you need to do is move one spot to create a Key Connection where business then gets a whole lot easier.

Now you know how strong your connections are, the next section will show you how you can increase their strength so you can move closer to key connections (if they aren't already there).

h) Leverage Points and Circles of Influence

'It's not about how much money you're making today, it's about what you're worth. What's your potential price tag out in the market? I say market value is a combination of RESULTS + REPUTATION + NETWORK. So if you're not constantly improving the work you do and the people you know and the brand you've created for yourself, then your market value goes down. But if you're pushing it, whether you stay in the same company or you move to a different one or you start your own, that's when you're going to have the maximum portable equity.'

- Sally Hogshead

In this section we will be showing you what to look for so you can uncover the leverage points and circles of influence in your network. Every network has them; it's only a matter of getting that fresh perspective on what they look like and where the opportunities lie.

WHAT IS A LEVERAGE POINT?

Leverage Points are the people in your network that have the potential to:

› Open doors for you;

› Lead to other door openers;

› Introduce you to industries or people with expertise you need/want;

› Provide referrals or introductions to you;

› Know specific people that you would like to connect with; and

› Willingly share like-minded connections, where you can add value to each other, create some kind of joint venture or exchange databases.

┌───┐
│ [!] **After looking at your Strategic Wealth Network and the participants within** |
│   **it, who is missing? Describe them or the skills you are looking for.** |
│   See page 86 of your *Connecting Mum Entrepreneurs Training Manual* for this exercise. |
└───┘

WHAT IS A CIRCLE OF INFLUENCE?

A set of keys is exactly like your network. Think about your set of keys, with each key representing one connection. A set of keys often has a lot of keys on it, a lot of connections. Holding all the keys together is the key ring. This is a circle of influence.

They are characterised by having a lot of keys/connections within their network. They are the natural promoters, the cheerleaders that can influence a large group of people. They want to tell the world. They naturally influence groups, are seen as trusted advisors and referrers, everyone likes them and they naturally attract a crowd.

Both of these points have something in common. The strength of your leverage points and the circles of influence that you identify are determined by what you know about them, their expertise, the relationship you have with them and the amount of trust you share. This also relates back to the strength of your connections.

HOW TO IDENTIFY THEM IN YOUR NETWORK?

Identifying leverage points and circles of influence in your Connection Map is essential to maximising your business growth through your network. So how do you identify them in your current Connection Map?

The power is in the information or knowledge you have about the groups or individuals. Here are some questions we would ask ourselves when determining where leverage points and circles of influences lie.

Think about a specific goal or outcome you have for your business. The way you reach that goal or outcome faster is by identifying commonalities with people in your network, that have the ability to help you, but preferably help each other. The way to find these similarities is by asking questions about some of the intermediate, advanced and key connections in your network.

Questions like:

› Who do they know?

› Where do they have influence?

› What industries do they associate with, have worked in or have links to?

› What do they love doing and is it relevant to what you are trying to achieve?

› What hobbies, sports or schools are they involved with?

› What states or countries have they worked in?

› What special skills, expertise or natural talents do they have?

The core skill involved in leverage points and circles of influence is getting to know people, engaging in relaxed conversation, listening to them closely and letting yourself be guided by a genuine interest in them. This is where the gold nuggets of information are shared and the magic of your network unfolds.

The next steps are:

1. Working out whom you should be building the relationships with, your leverage points and circles of influence within your current network, in the above manner.

2. In doing this, you will discover where the gaps are in your network. These are the spots where you know you need someone with skills or expertise, but you don't know anyone who matches it.

3. Then you can ask your Key Connections if they know people that can fill those gaps for you.

i) *1-Away* Connections

> 'Discovery consists of looking at the same thing as everyone else and thinking something different.'
> - **Albert Szent-Györgyi**

Now you have an understanding of leverage points and circles of influence you are ready for the *1-Aways*... this is where you raise your understanding to where you are only ever one connection away from the one you need or want. As you look back to your Connection Map, you will no doubt start to see the enormous amount of potential right in front of you. This gets taken to a higher level in the *1-Aways*.

If you look at your map, each person you wrote down also has a network. This person's contacts are your *1-Aways*. Let's say you have decided to design and manufacture soccer guernseys. Your immediate connections and family have supported you by buying just one to have some fun. You would like to receive some bulk orders. Whilst out with your friend Bob, who is wearing one of your guernseys, you meet Fred, one of Bob's friends. Fred happens to be a coach for a soccer team (see example below). He loved the design and wanted to know where they came from. This is the lead-in for you to introduce your product or service. This is the power of a *1-Away* connection.

These *1-Aways* are a gold mine for expanding your network, as you know someone with whom you have rapport, who has a direct link to that *1-Away* connection.

EXAMPLE OF 1-AWAY CONNECTIONS

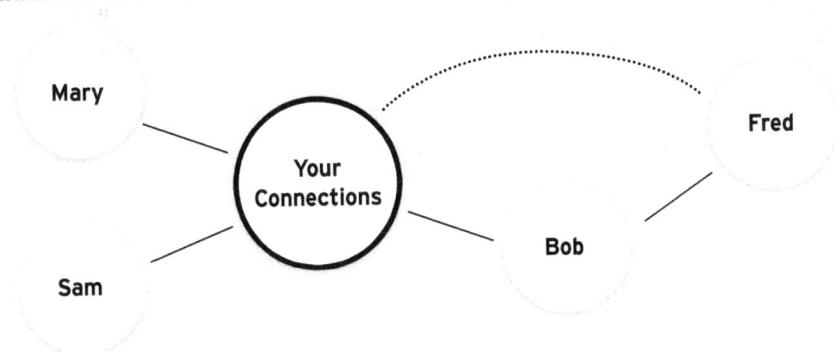

Mary

Your Connections

Fred

Bob

Sam

You will no doubt notice that it can be rather difficult to find these *1-Away* connections, as their very nature makes them tricky to uncover. You never know who is in somebody else's network! The best way to leverage this, that we have found, is to identify them by going through your circles of influence and your leverage points. Depending on your relationships with these people, they may or may not be comfortable with opening up their network to you. You will find that some people will guard their network like Alcatraz, whereas other people will be more than happy to put all their cards on the table.

We don't need to tell you which one is easier to work with.

So what are your action steps for this section?

1. Your priority needs to be building the relationship between your circles of influence and leverage points. *They can't help you if they don't know enough about you and you can't help them if you don't know enough about them.*

2. Asking for someone's network is a bit like asking if you can see them naked on a first date or asking to see their bank balances. *So it is up to them if they want to offer/share.*

3. A great way to jump over the obstacle just mentioned is by adding value to the connection that you would love to open up their network. This means, open up your network to help them. *More often than not you will find that they will do the same to help you out.* (This was covered in Chapter 1 in the section on *The 4 Laws of Connecting*)

> **!** Jot your thoughts and action steps down here so you can easily refer back to them. Also put a date next to each action, this is the date by which the action will be completed.
>
> See page 88 of your *Connecting Mum Entrepreneurs Training Manual* for this exercise.

j) Keeping Track and In Touch

'It is 6-7 times more expensive to acquire a new customer than it is to keep a current one.'
- **White House Office of Consumer Affairs**

'5-20% probability of selling to a new prospect.
60-70% probability of selling to an existing customer.'
- **Marketing Metrics**

Connecting Mum Entrepreneurs is about much more than just collecting business cards; however, that is the first step. As discussed in a tip further up, I use a lever arch business card binder to keep track and in touch with all my connections. What use is a bunch of names on a piece of paper if you don't know what they do, where they live or how to get in touch with them? The binder solves all those issues. You can also use a simple Excel spread sheet or a map on the wall.

These are really funky and fun ways to visualise all your connections. It is great as a memory jogger, rather than just having it in an Excel spreadsheet, particularly if you are more visually inclined like I am.

Now that you have a completed connection map, it's time to collect their contact details, if you don't already have them. Spend some time organising them by industry type, name, and job title or put them in the order of how they appear on your connection map (however your prefer really).

Or use one of the many apps that you can get for your smart phone to do this for you if that is your preference.

Keeping in touch with your connections is vital. I have talked about how to connect effectively and what you can do to increase your connection strength. If you don't keep in touch and connect properly with others, that connection strength fades and loses value to the point of having to start from scratch. Staying in touch can be as simple as having a coffee, connecting with multiple people at an event, or at work. This isn't about catching up with all your connections every single month, but being smart about the vehicles you use to connect (e.g. sending an e-mail with great content for that person around their interests, add comments on their posts on LinkedIn etc. Engage with them, let them know you care by sharing in their conversations online. There are many books on how to regularly connect; source which methods work best for you.

This subject can quite easily be an entire workshop in itself and changes regularly as technology changes so fast these days. I share many of the newest tools and apps as they come out and I start using them right away, so connect with me.

! **Now that you have a completed connection map, it's time to collect their contact details.**
Spend some time organising them by industry type, name, and job title
See page 99 of your *Connecting Mum Entrepreneurs Training Manual* for this exercise.

CONNECTING ENTREPRENEURS/MUMPRENEURS

After you have learnt the essentials about how to build up an effective network that can serve your business and consists of people that your business can serve, it's time to implement all you have learnt. This is done by asking the same question for each one of your connections:

'Can this person help me overcome a challenge?
Can I help them overcome a challenge?'

You go through all the people in your network and ask these questions about them. If yes to either, then you work out what you're going to share with them. If no, then you'll move onto the next person in your network and repeat the process.

People do business with and help people they know, like and trust. People love having challenges and problems solved... even if they are just small ones. This builds trust and creditability that elevates you. We talk about adding value to your network later in the book. Knowing what you have to offer someone makes truly connecting with them easier in the long run as you are coming with the intention of giving first that can lead to reciprocity.

Reciprocity can lead to collaborative partnerships (Joint Ventures), which is where business growth really hits the turbo charger and takes off.

TEAMWORK AND COLLABORATION

Once you've mapped out your network and identified those people who can potentially help you move things ahead quickly, you figure out how you can add value and team up or collaborate with them.

Collaboration is where two or more people or businesses come together to create something or simply add value to each other. It has never been more important to create results faster, than it is now. The pie is not limited, but technology and innovation are happening so fast that if you don't feel the urge to keep up with current trends and define the future, your business won't be relevant in a few years.

The following are a few examples from my own experiences. These are some of the joint ventures that I have been able to see grow to fruition.

ACCOUNTANT AND BUSINESS COACH

They both have similar clients, but offer very different solutions to their clients' challenges. They solve different problems. One specialises in all things profit, loss and tax related; the other in business growth and systemisation. By sharing their specific skills with each other's clients, they add value to their clients, at the same time increasing exposure to new leads and clients. As an example they could run an information event together and each invite their top ten clients.

HAIRDRESSER AND FASHION JEWELLER

Again both would have similar clients. Ladies love getting their hair done and we all like accessories to make us feel really special.

The salon has display stands of the jewellery for sale, while the jeweller provides a cut to the hairdressing salon of each sale.

To maximise this even more into an easy collaborative partnership, they created a Pamper Night, got the jeweller to showcase her products and how to dress them up for specific functions or dress styles, while inviting the local café to come and do the catering. They brought in a makeup artist to do a demonstration. Each business owner invited five guests and all the businesses present met new potential clients.

Remember you are more likely to increase your opportunity of selling to an existing customer, on average, by 60-70%, EVEN if they are someone else's EXISTING customers. The above example demonstrates that your selling opportunity will increase dramatically under the right circumstances.

* * *

Yes it is that easy to grow your businesses, you just need to discover where to start and that's what this book is about. Understand WHO is in your network.

The best way to speed up business growth is through collaborations. This is not a short cut; it simply multiplies exponentially what you could have achieved by yourself. Put your heads together with someone else that understands you, such as another mum or another female friend in business that you connect with. Work together and move forward in a wave of momentum. One person can't do everything, so collaborate with the right person and you can move mountains in your business and theirs.

This could be a friend or a relative; you might even be surprised when you do go through your network and evaluate each person for the types of interesting relationships that can grow into opportunities that will come seemingly out of nowhere.

ADDING
Value

ADDING *Value*

'Position yourself as a centre of influence, the one who knows the movers and shakers. People will respond to that, and you'll soon become what you project.'
- Bob Burg

a) Overcoming the Fear and the Stress of Connecting

Overcoming the fear and stress of connecting and networking is easy with the right knowledge and actions.

To be a great connector you need to understand yourself, this in itself can be a great journey of discovery; we need to understand people and how similar we all are. Most importantly, we need to learn how to add value and create a value-adding culture in what we do.

Adding value massively increases the connection between two people. It allows your connections to grow at a much faster rate. When people add value, it is natural to want to reciprocate and repay the favour. The more you add value the faster your connections grow and the closer you are to living an extraordinarily connected life.

So what are some great ways to add value and BE yourself? This means doing something that is originally you, not some recycled ideas or tactics that are common knowledge.

> 'You can't be successful when you cling to obsolete situations out of fear.
> Only when you put yourself out there wholeheartedly can the best opportunities present themselves.'
> **- Sally Hogshead**

Once you've understood yourself, who you are and what you do, it's much easier to be confident in yourself and your abilities. You let go being needy towards others and learn to have fun in what you do and how you connect to other people.

b) Effective Communication and Confidence

> 'The most beautiful thing you can wear is confidence.'
> **- Blake Lively**

> 'When you have confidence, you can have a lot of fun.
> And when you have fun, you can do amazing things.'
> **- Joe Namath**

The way in which we communicate, by being in the moment with a connection is an easy way to add value. This means being 100% attentive.

Keep comfortable eye contact and a smiling face. Not off in the clouds somewhere or running through some scenario in your head that has happened previously or you want to happen in the future. Be right there and connect with the person in front of you.

c) Effective Listening

When people don't listen to you – and we have all experienced this – it feels very different, doesn't it? We feel unwanted, insignificant and under-valued.

By simply listening and making people feel significant, in an open and honest way, this is impacting and will help you to stand out in a crowd. All great listeners stand out and you can too. Simply listen and be with the person and give your attention without expectation.

When you talk with someone and they respond, that is your queue to shut up and listen to every word. Why do we say this?

1. You find out about their passions and interests.

2. You find out about their family values and the way in which they live their life.

3. You find out about their motivations. Just watch their eyes light up, and their facial expressions change as they talk about something they enjoy.

People often give you much more information than you ask for. It will be missed if you don't listen intently.

Here are the reasons why:

› People are more likely to listen to us when we have honestly and intently listened to them.

› People pay more attention to information that is relevant to their point of view and circumstances. When you listen effectively, you discover their point of view and can talk with them accordingly.

Increasing the quality of your connections isn't about fishing for gold. This system is about connecting genuinely and confidently with other mums in business and helping each other to become more successful.

TAKING NOTICE

You can tell a lot about a person based on what they wear; how they present themselves, their office and even the way they set up their desk. Taking notice of these things puts you ahead of most people and allows you to pin point their passions, family values and the way they live their life in general. You can't know everything about them by this alone, but it does give you an insight and a massive advantage.

The advantage comes through striking up conversations on topics of mutual interests. It allows you to chat to them as a friend, not as someone you have just met and have no idea what they are interested in.

You build rapport by finding common ground, not opposing views. We are naturally attracted to other people that are just like us in some way. If you have nothing in common, no mutual interests, then the conversation usually won't last long… at least comfortably anyway.

Ask questions around a topic they have an interest in, and run with the conversation from there. You will be very surprised at how far it takes you. It is one thing to talk about the above topics, but observation without listening to what the other person is saying won't get you anywhere.

....

Story - A Lesson from Nature

Let me demonstrate how simple adding value is and the significant impact it has with a story from nature. Have you ever seen leaves dance?

This was a personal experience whilst on a 10-day silent Vipassana meditation in the Queensland hinterlands, a truly superb way to find yourself and reconnect. Yes, I did say TEN-day silent meditation!

The surroundings were beautiful, green, lush, picturesque rolling landscapes with views of a mountain that looked like an old volcano keeping an eye on us all. During a rest period from meditating, I was wandering around the parklike surroundings, towards the back of the property, when it started to rain.

Surrounding me were green lawns, landscaped gardens, the hinterland forest beyond the fence line and a selection of large trees dotted through the lawn area.

It was day three, so my mind had slowed; I was more present in the moment, so to speak, just enjoying, being aware.

As the rain came down in fine sheets. I took shelter under a nearby veranda. Standing there I heard *kercher, kercher*... It was a very unusual noise. I stood still, listening, looking for the source. *Kercher, kercher, kercher, kercher*... What I SAW was leaves dancing! Leaping in the air, one after the other. *Kercher, kercher*...

What was causing the leaves to dance and jump in the air is a perfect example of adding value, from nature. On the outside of this large tree canopy the rain was falling in sheets. You know the sort; you get really wet, really quickly.

On the lush green grass under this particular tree were dried, curled up, brown fallen leaves; many of them just lying there scattered underneath the branches.

The raindrops were running down the outermost leaves, and then dripping onto the inner leaves. As they ran down the leaves, they joined together making larger, weightier raindrops, creating more momentum and speed. One droplet joining forces with many more; all of them adding value to the next, until finally they would reach the lowest leaf and drip off, falling to the grassy earth below.

But many of the now larger, united drops would hit a dried, curled up leaf and the sheer size and weight of the water would cause the leaf to jump in the air. *Kercher, kercher*... One after the other. *Kercher, kercher, kercher*... leaves dancing in unison, simply due to one raindrop adding value to another. A single raindrop would not have affected the leaves, but many of them did and the sheer number that had added value caused me to witness leaves dancing; many of them! *Kercher, kercher, kercher*... Leaping and dancing into the air.

Have you seen leaves dance in your daily activities or even in the past?

· ·

RORY'S LEMONADE STAND – HOW HE WOULD GROW HIS BUSINESS

In Chapter 2: *Mapping Out Your Connections,* we touched on my son Rory's networks and connections. Now with everything we have learnt, let's look at a business that Rory decided to start one day when he was six and see how he could use everything we have looked at to his advantage.

At that time Rory had an affinity with LEGO. The week before that it was BIONICLE, but then it was LEGO. As any parent knows, toy costs aren't exactly cheap when there is a collection or a set they are after! So I discussed with Rory that I wasn't going to fund any more LEGO and if he wanted more he would have to fund it himself.

He decided to start up a lemonade stand and sell as much as possible to buy all his LEGO. Who could he have gone to if he wanted to get his business off the ground and growing as fast as possible? He could have called 465 people (that all love sugary lemonade) before he even needed to consider running any kind of external marketing or advertising. He had lots of rapport with his friends so they were intermediate to advanced connections and they were more than happy to come and support him and buy lemonade.

Let's just stop for a moment and think about the strategy behind this. Rory is focussing on one connection at a time in order to get his sales. There is no doubt this is very effective, but surely there is a better way to leverage his results. What if Rory was to focus on bulk sales?

If Rory has 465 connections then that is more than one birthday for every day of the year. There is bound to be a few birthday parties that he can tap into so he can get some bulk orders, wouldn't you agree?

There are also the natural promoters and cheerleaders, the kids that spread the word like wildfire. These kids might even want to help Rory in his lemonade stand. Isn't it possible that Rory's friends also have friends that like and want to buy lemonade? Suddenly, he no longer has access to just 465 people, but 465 plus his friends' networks of people.

As the lemonade stand took off, he found that all his time was being taken up by his new business and that his schoolwork was starting to suffer. What could he do? Does that sound like anyone you might know? Instead of schoolwork suffering it might be family.

So he decided to ask other kids to sell the lemonade for him and he sold only bulk lemonade to his distributors. He has all the right knowledge to make them all a lot of money so they can all go and sell lemonade. This is where those natural promoters and cheerleaders may want to have a piece of the action. Rory, an average kid, knows 465 people, so let's say that all his distributors know the same amount of people. He can train them to map their network and show him the strategies he used to get his business growing quickly and before you know it, he has a very formidable sales team.

Best of all, their overheads are low because they are not doing formal advertising like everyone else, they are using the best marketing tool around... their connections and word of mouth.

THE Wow FACTOR

THE *Wow* FACTOR

a) Connecting Above and Beyond

Have you had people that have wowed you in the past with a little unexpected added value service, an act of kindness, or something that impacted you positively? Of course, we all have, but for most of us it can seem like a long time ago.

It is so much more fun and impacting to add value and be connected. Putting yourself in a position to play more together, share and empower others, creating a ripple effect with great stories that make people think differently, cause paradigm shifts and change things for the better.

Here's a restaurant example. The standard restaurant experience is one that roughly goes like this: you call the restaurant and make a booking, arrive at the restaurant, eat dinner, then pay the bill. Traditionally the experience isn't one that is largely different between restaurants. What if you called the restaurant, made your booking and the receptionist asks you for all the names of your guests and says there will be a surprise waiting for you?

Then, on the day you are booked in, you receive an SMS saying, 'Hi, Fred! Really looking forward to seeing you tonight. The Chef has created some VERY special desserts for you tonight, too!'

When you arrive at the restaurant, there are helium balloons with the names of all your guests beautifully printed on them, indicating where everyone is sitting. Then when it comes to paying for the bill, they hand you the black American Express folder, you pay with your credit card and give the folder back to the waitress. Once they have processed the payment, they return the black folder to you. You open it and see your credit card with a small envelope, which says on the front, 'We really want to thank you...' So of course you open it. It has a little note inside, which reads, 'Every time you dine with us, a hungry child gets fed. Thank you from them and from us too.'

This is adding value at its best. What could be better than having a great meal at a restaurant, and at the same time knowing that you have made feeding a hungry child possible?

This is something that restaurants don't need to do but it adds value to their clients in a big way. In a 'connected way' you all would have FELT that connection, just by listening to the words of the story.

That the restaurant shares the experience of giving with their customers is the unexpected 'WOW' moment, something that is of value to the person receiving it. This makes it that much more appreciated. Plus we've all ordered a 'very special dessert'! An upsell suggested very elegantly before we even arrived at restaurant.

b) Staying True to Yourself

'We each have the potential to do something beyond our wildest imagination.
As long as we're prepared to make it happen.'
- **Sally Hogshead**

'Remembering that you are going to die is the best way I know to avoid the trap of thinking you have something to lose. You are already naked.
There is no reason not to follow your heart.'
- Steve Jobs

Okay, but what if the little voice in your head is saying, 'Yeah, but I don't feel comfortable using that approach or that doesn't suit my personality.'

Then the distinction that I would like to make here is that it's not about you becoming someone different or using different words, it's about exploring other options that work really well for you. Be open and honest with your nature. It's about you making things yours, owning them in your own unique way; using your words, your intonations.

In your cheeky, fun or your professional, quietly spoken manner it's about being a new improved better version of you, but still being you. That's what people like and want; not a cardboard cut out of someone else.

c) Giving Without Expectation

'The heart that gives, gathers.'
- Marianne Moore

This can be a tough one to master. This means no score keeping. Meet people with no expectations in mind. This not only relieves the pressure of high performance, but also means you are there to add value to the person you are meeting. Naturally, what goes around comes around. We are all human beings and we naturally want to help others, it is hardwired as much as you may not want to admit it, so dig deep and give generously. Having no expectations allows your mind to be open to any and all opportunities, no blinkers.

PURPOSE AND PASSION DISCOVERY

> What do you want most out of life? A1........................., A2.........................
> What do you want for this planet? B1........................., B2.........................
> What makes you special? C1........................., C2.........................
> What can you do today? D1........................., D2.........................

Now place your answers in the blank spaces below:

Scenario

I will (D1) .... using my (C1) .... to achieve

(B1) .... so will achieve (A1) ....

> [!] **What is your Purpose and Passions? Complete the scenario!**
> See page 101 of your *Connecting Mum Entrepreneurs Training Manual* for this exercise.

You may need to round out the edges in each scenario so it makes complete sense. The magic in this exercise is that the results are hidden until the end so your brain cannot jump ahead and figure out the answer you think it should be.

In our experience, most people that express what they do by relating it back to their above answers have a radical change in their body language, facial expressions and energy. Before it seemed like 'going through the motions', whereas afterwards it feels like a heartfelt response, full of enthusiasm and excitement, highlighting that this person has a true passion for what they do.

We hope you found this exercise useful and choose to use your phrases in some way. Try expressing what you do with someone close, using your above answers. Watch their reaction.

YOUR OWN UNIQUENESS

To understand what uniqueness is, let's first describe what it is not. When people go to courses, workshops, seminars and the like, they often come home and act like a cardboard cut out of someone else. This is imitating someone else's uniqueness, not your own.

True connections are created by the essence of people
and your own uniqueness

Allowing your *Uniqueness* or your *Giftedness* to run wild is where you will be most in flow, where things are the easiest and you can be 100% totally unashamedly yourself. If it isn't comfortable for you to show your uniqueness then this is something you really need to work on. That way you can use your uniqueness to your advantage instead of treating it like an annoying monkey on your back.

Your 'Why' and your Uniqueness/Giftedness help you go from the hesitant and unconfident kid on the left to the ecstatic and excited kid on the right:

1. What are the things that make you unique?
   They could be quirks or specific skill sets that you have.
   (If you get stuck, ask your partner or a Key Connection.)

2. What can you do to start using your uniqueness in your business/career, if you don't already? Or what can you do to leverage your uniqueness even more than what you are already doing?

> **!** **What are the things that make you unique?**
> **What can you do start using your uniqueness in your business/career?**
> See page 104 of your *Connecting Mum Entrepreneurs Training Manual* for this exercise.

d) Bringing It All Together Mindset

How many people do you now know?

Connections, and more importantly strong connections, are designed to make your life easier; they open doors that are usually closed. They get you into places where the hard sell won't. Every single person has hundreds of potential connections to positively affect everyone around them. We have seen that even a 5-year-old, has 465 people in his network. It's time for you to step up and connect effectively with yours and add value to everyone around you.

Connecting effectively gives you the most exhilarating life you could ever imagine. It turns every day into a play day. Knowing you have many, many people around you that you can help and can help you through tough situations is a truly awesome and fulfilling feeling.

It only takes one connection to change your life forever and they are often hidden in plain sight, where you least expect them to be. This is the person that can rocket your business to new heights, expand globally or provide you with the tools to get your health and fitness or relationships to where you want them to be.

Many of these 'plainly in sight' connections hide in the *1-Away* category, easy to miss, but sitting right in front of you.

Who is in plain sight for you, that you have now discovered, or think you might have discovered?

What if you had access to Richard Branson, Warren Buffet or Donald Trump? These people and people like them can tip your world on its head with what you think you know and propel you into success with the snap of a finger. That is the ultimate power of connecting!

Define whom you need and expect they will show up! *When the student is ready the teacher will appear.* One thing is for sure… people are everywhere, so soon enough you will find the connection you are after.

Once you have finished reading these last few pages, make an action list and kick some serious butt!

e) Living the Example

'Our lives are defined by opportunities, even the ones we miss.'
- F. Scott Fitzgerald

You develop great rapport through listening, responding, being confident with and adding value to others. These traits can easily turn into great long-term relationships and key connections. Amazing opportunities, collaborations and joint ventures can be discovered right under your nose, when you connect with people in the right way and add value, it becomes a reciprocal relationship that unites individuals, communities and the world.

What do we do at *Business Mums Solutions* is add value to our clients and people we meet on a daily basis.

At the outset there are a few things I do in particular. Right from the way I greet people, it sets the stage. It's my nature to jump all over people, giving hugs left, right and centre. This is usually combined with some funny comment, like 'Hello, gorgeous young man!' I smile, I'm bubbly and people tell me I'm a joy to be around. I attract people to me and they want to know more about me and how I help mums in business. They want to know what I'm on! I often tell them I'm full of joy.

From research, I have found that 87% of business is done through connections. I know within less than two minutes of meeting someone, whether they are utilising their network of connections effectively or if they understand that 87% of business comes from connections.

If not, I will immediately add value to what they are doing by suggesting ideas to increase their business by leveraging their connection base, saving them time with a new app or suggesting they connect with someone specific that may be in the room.

Is 87% of your business coming through your connections? Use this book as a tool to discover and capture this huge chunk of business.

I care. Mums are used to being the nurturer and in many cases, they are not used to being nurtured. That's why I make a difference to people's lives and work hard to stand out.

SERVICES WE OFFER

TRAININGS AND WORKSHOPS

Introductory and Accelerated Trainings on *Partnering for Profit and Personal Positioning*.

These programmes will help you:

> Discover how to generate more leads, fast growth and build your reputation as a key person of influence and success.

> Open up new markets whilst using leverage and having fun.

> Stand up and out. Identify your target collaborator and market, their desires, fears and mistakes so you can assist yourself and your partners.

> Discover your hidden untapped value that others want and need.

> Define your strategic network and bring the team together.

> Understanding the Credibility Loop and how to improve it for your success.

> Eliminating failure by not going too big too soon.

> The easy steps of securing collaborative partnerships and simple joint ventures.

> What the agreement needs to look like and how to confirm who is doing what and when.

> How to ensure continued success.

> Managing and understanding expectations and communication plans.

COACHING - PERSONAL AND PERFORMANCE

We will bring all the topics and fundamentals from all of the workshops and trainings on *Collaborative Partnering for Profit* and *Personal Positioning*.

We overcome the 4 common challenges for women in business:

› Undervaluing ourselves and our products.

› Going round in circles chasing time, opportunities and customers that don't work out.

› Being nearly unknown. In other words you don't have enough customers that know about you.

› Being a stressed-out soloist who is worn out, has had enough and is uninspired.

PLUS, as a Practitioner in NLP Coaching, Time Line Therapy™ and Hypnosis, this assists me to encourage my clients' self-expression to be the best it can be. This way you will be fully equipped to turn your business and your life around.

AREAS I SPECIALISE IN:

› Modelling for Excellence - dissolving Guilt and Procrastination whilst gaining Clarity and Motivation to create the life you truly want and deserve

› Collaborative Partnerships

› Personal Positioning - Building your Reputation and Value

› Success and Performance Strategies

Happy business, happy mum, having fun, happy kids, great profit.

SPEAKING

Sally has experienced first hand the stress, overwhelm and worry that can engulf women when they're trying to do it all and is deeply passionate about helping, inspiring and teaching women to grow great businesses, while they raise amazing kids.

Please call Sally to discuss your next event and how she can assist with practical instructions and words of inspiration.

CONNECTING CIRCLES

One of my favourite types of networking events are 'connecting parties'. These are parties where I get the opportunity to claim bragging rights for all the mums I do business with. I organise parties to showcase mums businesses to VIPs who have been specifically invited, as they are the perfect clients for the mums I work with. These events provide alliances and immeasurable growth opportunities for the business owners I connect.

The atmosphere is relaxed, fun and casual. I engineer an environment where people can truly connect in a non-threatening way. As time goes on in today's increasingly chaotic world, people seem to be having less fun (just walk down the street and count how many people are really smiling…). My live events bring magic to the room, as all great events seem to do. It doesn't feel like a business event on the night, but people consistently tell me they are amazed at what the event can create for their business success. The virtual circle events still have the same excitement and collaborative spirit but are created in a more special manner. Attend one to find out!

KEYNOTE SPEECHES

Over the last several years, I have been asked to provide keynote speeches (over sixty minute presentations) for different events. I have had the pleasure to give an audience a taste of what is sitting right under their noses. If you organise events then I would be more than happy to give a keynote speech for you and I will tailor each speech to suit your audience.

The topics that I have covered and love speaking on are:

› Business Development

› Customer Service

› Joint Ventures

› Involving Our Children in Business and Setting Them Up for Future Success

ABOUT THE AUTHOR

Sally A Curtis helps overwhelmed, frustrated mums in business.
For heaps of FREE resources check out her website
www.BusinessMumsSolutions.com
Sharing is Sally's way to HELP mums just like her.

Sally has built **Business Mums Solutions** from the ground up, where you will find heaps of information on building great businesses, growing great kids and saving time, so you have 'me' time, as well. Sally has shared a lot of great information in this book for mums in business and continues to share tools and resources on her blog, website, social media sites, seminars and live trainings.

Sally exists to share as much of her wisdom, skills, tools and stories as she can to help mums in business. She is all about simplicity (Sally loves all things Apple) and saving time is her strongest driver. If Sally can share a tool or resources that gives you more time to spend with your family; or a new strategy to grow your business more effectively, then her heart will sing.

If she can inspire you with stories on how to enrol your kids in your business and vision; or inspire you to keep going, then she has achieved one of her greatest goals.

If you're out of the start-up phase then Sally will help you with the next fastest way to grow through simple Joint Ventures. She will use her skills to help you so don't hesitate to contact Sally today.

Sally has started several of her own businesses from scratch, because 'they sounded like a good idea at the time'. She has poured her heart into business: her blood, sweat, tears and tantrums... and made each business work. She has done this with an 18-month old who is now 12. She had fun along the way.

Sally is also a keen investor. Through her eyes she looks at business and people as an investment in our futures. Sally is an advocate of making mutual decisions, keeping an eye on the numbers, making it happen, and growing great kids by leading by example.

Sally's two most favourite quotes are:
'When the student is ready, the teacher will appear.'
'Opportunities are a daily occurrence and often hidden in plain sight.'

Sally has over 20 years of business development experience across a variety of industries ranging from cosmetics, to retail, media and events and franchising.

She has worked for well-known companies including: Aussie Farmers Direct, Val Morgan, McCain Foods and Clinique, plus alongside many outstanding entrepreneurs. Sally has always contributed to the growth of organisations through developing new business, leveraging existing relationships and implementing strategic initiatives. She loves to see business and growth made simple.

Sally has spent a number of years as a consultant to various global events organisations, ensuring that the events are well attended and run effectively, making significant profit margins.

Some of Sally's previous clients include:
Dale Beaumont - CEO of Dream Express International Pty Ltd
Duane Alley - Founder and CEO of Performance Results Pty Ltd
Mike Handcock - Chairman and Founder of Rock Your Life Global
Dr Joanna Martin - Founder of One of Many and Shift Enterprises UK
Shaune Clarke - Founder of 6 Figure Speaker Training and Big Brand Speaking

NOTES

NOTES

NOTES

NOTES

www.ingramcontent.com/pod-product-compliance
Lightning Source LLC
Chambersburg PA
CBHW052017230326

41598CB00078B/3528